HOW TO MAKE MONEY TEACHING ONLINE

Eric Frick

Published by Eric Frick 2019.

Updated 3/6/19

Dedication

This book is dedicated to my Father Roy K. Frick. He was a great inspiration in my life and a role model for everyone who knew and worked with him. Although he passed away in 2008, his influence on his family, students and co-workers will leave a lasting legacy.

Contents

10

Foreword

Hello and welcome to the book! I published my first class online on the Udemy platform in 2016. I had many trials and tribulations along the way it was challenging work for me to complete this class even though I had considerable teaching experience and knew the material very well. I remember finishing this class in the September timeframe and had to wait a few days for the Udemy staff to review and approve the course for publication.

After the class went live, I did not have any sales, and I feared that any real students would never see my material.

After some Internet research, I decided to post some free coupons on a well-known website for you Udemy students. Several hours later I discovered that ten people had signed up for my class with the free coupon. I decided to text my best friend and excitedly told him that ten people had signed up for the course. I quickly had to text him again a few minutes later to say to him that the number was now 15. This continued for several hours, and I was also getting a confirmation email for each student that was signing up for the class. By the end of the weekend, when the dust has settled I had over 1300 students sign up for my class.

Although I had not made any money from the free coupons that I had given out, I realized there was a significant demand for the type of material that I was delivering. I have a background in software development, and it turns out this type of material is in tremendous demand on Udemy and platforms like it. I also realized that with hard work and patience, I could develop a series of classes around software development that could provide me with a monthly income that could supplement my day job.

I had been teaching in the evenings at several local universities in the Central Ohio area a few years before meet experimenting with online teaching. I really enjoyed the process of interacting with the students in teaching software development courses; however, the pay was not very good, and I had to work very long hours after a very exhausting and stressful full-time job that I had at the time. My goal for my online teaching business was to replace the income that I was making from teaching part-time in the evenings. At the time of the writing of this book, I have been able to achieve that goal.

I have also found that developing publishing of my online classes allows me much more freedom of expression than teaching part-time in the university environment. When you teach at a university, you're often limited by the material that is approved by the department that you're instructing in. When you develop your classes online or write books, you can publish any content that you are interested in without constraints. This comes at the cost of some difficult work to gather and publish your material on any given subject, however for me; the trade-off was worth it. I can now publish anything I want. Another advantage I found is that even though my expertise is in software development, I have developed so many new skills while starting the online publishing business that I have many more topics to blog about, post on my YouTube channel and write books.

I have learned so many things along the way, but I decided to write this book to help people that want to establish a business with online publishing and to help them not make some of the mistakes that I made along the way. I also want to share some of that knowledge with new and upcoming course authors. To get started in the online teaching business, you do not need a formal background in education to get started. You also don't need to be the world's greatest expert in the subject you intend to teach online. You do, however, need a passion for teaching and the genuine desire to deliver your students the best possible material that you can—given the constraints you have with time money and equipment.

In addition to being an opportunity to make money, teaching online can be very rewarding since you potentially have a worldwide reach with the power of the Internet. This business will require you to publish material regularly and to keep building your following on a bit by bit basis. Most probably you will not see wild overnight success. I hope that you do, but the reality is you will have to start slow and steadily build until you have met your goals, and probably exceed them if you stick with it. You will have slow sales cycles, and you will be tempted to give in. Try and learn from each, and every day. There are times to sit back and plan, and then there are times to crank out some content. You will find it is hard work, but very rewarding.

Small victories can be significant milestones in this type of business. I occasionally play golf with some of my buddies. One of my short-term goals was to make a sale while we were golfing. (Even if it was only $5 in revenue) It was just the thought that I could be making money while I was out playing. Well, it finally happened, and I think I celebrated after the round with a beer. (I would have done that anyway!) Next year, while we were playing, my buddies asked me why I was not feverishly checking my phone for sales. I told them since I had been doing this for a while I had now built a pipeline of daily sales and was pretty sure I had made some sales during the day. While I'm not trying to brag by making this statement—the key is through some very hard work, you can get predictable results, which is very rewarding.

Although I've met my initial goal of replacing my part-time teaching income, I still have not reached my long-term goal of being able to live off of my book royalties and monthly class payments. However, my business is still steadily growing, and I am learning new in exciting Technologies every day.

One of the enormous benefits in starting my online business presented me was someone who viewed some of my YouTube videos contacted me and asked if I was interested in becoming a full-time course author. After the interview process and discussing the opportunity, I decided to take the position, and I am now a full-time course Author at Linux Academy where I teach online cloud certification programs. If I had never started my online business or started my own

YouTube channel, I most probably would have never discovered that opportunity. By accepting that opportunity, I have now accomplished one of my life goals to become a full-time author and have the freedom to work in any location I desire. The job that I have now is incredibly fulfilling and financially rewarding. You can't ask for a better combination than that.

My suggestion to you if you're thinking about teaching online is to develop some short term and long term goals that will help you formulate your business strategy. It will also help you determine the resources you will need to devote to achieving those goals. I sincerely hope that some of the material in this book help you achieve your goals and allow you to build a successful business.

1 Why Teach Online?

"We never know which lives we influence, or when, or why.
Stephen King

Teaching online and online publishing is much easier today that is was just a few years ago. Many of the barriers of entry have been removed or lowered substantially. For example, a few years ago it was essential to have a high definition video camera in order to start producing good quality videos for online publication. Many people today have that capability on their phone that they already own. With a cell phone and some video editing software, you can get up and running right away.

As far as the publishing end of things, you can set up a free account with Amazon or a service like Draft to Digital and you can publish eBooks or print books with just a word processor. No longer do you need a publishing company to get started. I have been publishing on Amazon for the last couple of years and have found the process extremely gratifying, in addition to helping me develop a nice side income.

I will warn you that if your primary motivation is making large amounts of money quickly, this is probably not the right opportunity for you. You can make a substantial amount of money teaching and publishing online, but it requires a lot of work and producing material on a very regular basis. You will learn along the way what methods and channels work the best for you and the only way to master this is through the experience of publishing quality material frequently.

Even though I might have tempered your expectations with the previous paragraph, publishing and teaching online has some unbelievable advantages as compared to other jobs such as:

- You can work literally anywhere in the world, and perhaps the only thing you need is an internet connection.
- You can be your own boss and set your own working hours. I have found that working on a regular basis and chipping away at a large project works better for me than binge working.
- You really don't have a boss in the self-publishing business so you can plot your own course and march to your own drum. You will have to answer to your subscribers and customers in terms of reviews and sales, but ultimately you can publish whatever material you want.

- The market for ebooks and online classes is huge and the market is growing. There are many publishing and teaching opportunities online that you can tap into.
- You can start part-time with this opportunity and work as much as you want. You can start of using this to supplement your income and at the point where you are comfortable you can then move to do this full-time.
- The last major advantage is that you don't need a large amount of equipment to get started. If you only want to publish books, you only need a word processor and a computer to begin. To work with video, you can get started with just a cell phone and some video editing software.

In summary, this is a great time to enter this market. Although there is a lot of competition since there are already so many authors publishing content online, this also means that there is a robust market for material that has already on the market. You can start small with this business and put in as much time as you desire. Throughout this book, I have included some tips that will hopefully make your transition into publishing, a smooth one.

2 How Much Money Can You Make?

"I never teach my pupils, I only attempt to provide the conditions in which they can learn."
Albert Einstein

I wish I could tell you that money is not critical and not to worry about it, but sadly that is not the case. I will also tell you that while I have not gotten rich by teaching online, I have built a steady recurring business that is steadily growing. By starting my online venture, I have had some opportunities that have been made available to me that I otherwise would not have had.

The market for online classes and self-publishing has been developing rapidly over the last decade. Services like Amazon KDP and online sites such as Udemy, have lowered the barrier of entry into these fields and have created a robust and vibrant market for online material. I follow many online course authors that have been extremely successful. In the next few paragraphs I will describe some of the top performers in this business and the incredible amounts of money they have made online. After that, I will present some of the average statistics from some of the online platforms to show what the average author makes on various platforms.

The online market for courses has exploded in the last few years. Udemy which is one of the leading online course marketplaces boasts of having 24 million students and 80,000 classes online. Also, they state that they have over 35,000 instructors. Other sites such as Skillshare have over 3 million subscribers and over 25,000 classes. Sites such as these have created an enormous marketplace for course authors to sell online material.

The market is also strong for other types of digital products such as Ebooks and videos. Amazon Kindle Direct is the world largest publisher of ebooks, and it continues to grow year after year. Other publishing aggregators such as Draft to Digital and Smashwords make it very easy to self publish ebooks to a wide variety of online publishers such as Barnes and Noble, Apple's iBooks and others through a single simple interface. All of these channels add up to tremendous opportunities for authors and online publishers. I will describe all of the channels in more detail later in this book.

I published my first online class on Udemy in August of 2015. Since then I have followed some high profile, online instructors. Some of them have racked up some incredible statistics in terms of numbers of students and followers. I will give you a brief overview of some of these instructors to provide you with an idea of the ultimate upside of publishing classes online.

The first example I will describe is Phil Ebiner. Phil is the founder of Video School online and is one of the leading instructors on Udemy. If you look at his profile page on Udemy, it states that he has over 700,000 students with 88 published courses. I subscribe to one of his newsletter where he released his monthly earning reports. Most months Phil averages sales of $50,000 per month. Now please realize he is one of the top instructors in this field, and his sales are certainly not typical for most online instructors, but it does illustrate the high end of this field and if you can create quality content at a scale the type of income that is possible. You can see Phil's teacher profile here:

https://www.udemy.com/user/philipebiner2/

Another top instructor is Frank Kane who teaches data science classes. Frank is the founder of Sundog Education and a former engineer at Amazon. I recently saw a post from him that he crossed the $ 1 million sales mark on Udemy. He also publishes on other platforms as well such as Amazon and Skillshare. In fact, most online course authors publish on multiple channels which gives the best chance of maximizing sales and minimizing risk. I will talk more about this in later chapters as well. You can get more information about Sundog Education here:

https://sundog-education.com/

My last example is Rob Percival. Rob is one of the early Udemy instructors that teach web development. He currently has over 1 million students and has published 41 courses! That's a fantastic accomplishment. Even though he got in at the right time and was only of the early Udemy success stories, he illustrates the point of how strong the market demand can be for quality material that he delivered consistently. You can see Rob's profile here:

https://www.udemy.com/user/robpercival/

As for my income, I have been able to grow my business over the last few years from just a few dollars a week to substantial monthly income. As of the time of this writing, my business revenue has doubled over the previous year. To be clear, I am not in the class of some of the earlier instructors that I have mentioned, but I am delighted with the growth that I have achieved with my business and look forward to growing it further. Perhaps the most frustrating part of my business was the very beginning when sales were painfully slow, and it seemed that increasing it to a reasonable level would become an almost impossible task. By diversifying on to multiple channels, I was able to establish and much more repeatable monthly sales revenue. After that by increasing the amount of content on top of that led to substantial growth.

In summary, it is possible to make quite a bit of money publishing online video courses and books. You can find many examples of highly successful course authors that are earning an excellent income from publishing content online. Although you may not achieve the success have some of the industry leaders, you will undoubtedly be able to establish a repeatable successful online business with hard work and perseverance. There were many times that I wanted to throw in the towel and quit when things were difficult. I am satisfied with the effort that I have put in so far and have a great deal of satisfaction with the content that I have produced. I certainly hope you have a great deal of success in creating your online content!

3 Where Can I Teach?

"There is nothing happens to any person but what was in his power to go through with."
Marcus Aurelius

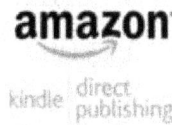

There are many platforms to deliver online content, and the list is growing every day. One of the great things about publishing online classes and books is you are not limited to a single platform. However, when you are first getting started, I think it is an excellent idea to narrow the list down to a single platform just to get started and get the ball rolling. In the following paragraphs, I will describe some of the most popular online learning platforms as well as some of their advantages and disadvantages. Ultimately you will, however, to try some of these for yourself to see which platforms suit your needs the best.

3.1 Udemy

One of the largest sites for online education is Udemy. This site boasts of having millions of students taking classes from over 80,000 instructors. There are courses for just about everything you can think of that is for sale on Udemy. Students on this site buy courses on an individual basis. Udemy is not a subscription type of service.

There is no fee to get started, and as an instructor, you fill out a simple application in addition to providing some banking information so that you can get paid. You set the pricing for classes on this platform, and you will get 50% of the revenue from a sale. Unfortunately, most courses on Udemy are sold during a sale. For $9.99 and you would get half of that which is approximately $5. under this agreement Udemy will help you market your course in exchange for the split of the revenue share. So for example, if you sell 100 courses in a month at $9.99, you would make approximately $500.

Udemy has gone through several pricing model changes over the years. Many of their initial instructors became fed up with the new pricing model and have left to sell courses on their websites. You can post courses on Udemy and not be in the revenue-sharing model and set your own prices. However, the likelihood of you selling courses under this model is minimal. If you are going to do that, you might as well host classes on your own site and market them yourself. One strategy you might consider is to sell smaller versions of your courses on Udemy and try to market those students to sell longer courses on your own website.

Another disadvantage of selling on Udemy is that you do not get the student's email addresses who are taking your courses. Udemy is also very restrictive about sending direct marketing messages to your students to outside platforms. The theory that Udemy has is that you will sell larger volumes of courses with such a large Marketplace. Udemy has sales almost every month, and if you post courses on Udemy, more than likely, you will generate some monthly revenue. However, to make a large amount of money, you'll have to make a large number of consistent sales.

3.2 Skillshare

Skillshare is another place that you can sell your online courses. Skillshare operates on a different model than Udemy and is a subscription-based service. Students pay approximately $10 a month to have access to skillshare, and with that subscription, they get access to all of the courses on Skillshare. Instructors get paid based on the number of minutes that their videos are watched. There is no fee to sign up for skillshare, and it is free to post classes in the marketplace. Also, skillshare does not review your courses; it is up to you to review your own content before posting it online.

Skillshare pays their instructors on the 16th of the month after the closing of the prior month. Also when you post a new course, it will not become visible to the General market place unless you have 20 students that have signed up for the class. In this initial phase, until you get 20 students, you need to have some marketing capability to get those first 20 sign-ups. You can generally get this reasonably quickly; however through the use of family friends and business contacts.

In addition to the minutes watched Skillshare also pays you $10 for every new student that signs up for the skillshare service. You can offer two free months of skillshare membership to new students to entice them to sign up for the service. This referral process is an excellent way to get additional revenue on Skillshare. Although you do not get student email addresses on Skillshare, they are much more lenient about direct student communication than Udemy is. Skillshare is by far my favorite platform to deliver content on it seems to be a much more relaxed environment, and I get better feedback for my students.

3.3 Teachable

If you don't want to conform to policies of a third party to post your courses you can use a site like Teachable to host your own courses online. Teachables lowest pricing tier starts at $29 a month, and they charge a 5% fee on each sale that you make. The user interface for teachable is straightforward to use, and the LMS system they use is pretty good for delivering online courses.

Teachable does not help with marketing and anyway driving traffic and getting students to sign up for your courses is entirely up to you. This process can be a daunting prospect for most new instructors. Also, there is no review process here you can post literally any type of content you want, and the pricing is entirely up to you. I have posted some links to teachable resources in the resources section of this book.

3.4 Thinkific

Another site that is similar to teachable is Thinkific. Thinkific does offer a free tier to get started, but they limit you to three courses. In addition, the free tier does not allow you to assign a custom domain name to your website. You will have to use a Thinkific URL for this. To have your domain name with Thinkific, you will have to upgrade to the base which is $29 a month and is very similar to the package on teachable. Teachable and Thinkific are very similar types of platforms that are very good for delivering course content, but neither of these packages provides any marketing support.

3.5 WordPress

Another option for delivering courses on your own platform is to utilize WordPress. WordPress offers several LMS themes that you can plug into a WordPress site to deliver courses as well as you lysing something like Woo Commerce to collect payment for online courses and ebooks. The advantage of utilizing WordPress is that it is entirely customizable and you can make the site look like anything you want–given enough time and effort.

The downside of this platform is that if you're not familiar with constructing WordPress sites, there is a fairly steep learning curve to be able to set up and customize your own LMS system without any experience. This customization will cut deeply into your course production time in the beginning if you decide to go this route. The advantage of taking this approach is that you can make your site look like anything you want–one that is highly customizable.

3.6 YouTube

YouTube Is the largest video website in the world. It is owned by Google and is the second largest search engine in the world behind the Google search engine. I think having a presence on YouTube is essential for online content authors. YouTube has almost unlimited potential as far as a top side for an online content author. Some of the top YouTubers make an incredible amount of money every year. The great thing about YouTube is that your videos will be watched twenty-four hours a day, 365 days a year to a worldwide audience.

Having said all of that, YouTube is packed with content and, there is a lot of competition to get views. I have found, however, that if you deliver quality content on a routine basis, your channel will grow very predictably. You can make money by selling ads on YouTube, and it's just a click when you post content. You won't make a lot of money doing this until you get a significant number of years to get regular additional income. However, there are other ways to make money on YouTube – the most prominent is to put links to advertise your online courses by posting coupons or discounts to your YouTube viewers.

Another way to make money on YouTube is to include affiliate marketing links to other products that might be part of your online course that you can recommend for people to buy. There is an unbelievable number of affiliate marketing programs on the web today where you can recommend all types of products and get a fee for each sale, based upon on your custom link for the recommendation. These products are highly dependent on the kind of content that you're delivering, but if there is a good fit for affiliate marketing, YouTube is an excellent vehicle to deliver these types of links.

You might also find that you can get customer prospects from YouTube based on the type of content that you're delivering as well. If people like your content, they will see you as an authority figure and seek you out for the type of business that you operate. The most challenging aspect of YouTube is that you need to produce content regularly to get your channel to grow consistently. This production effort is a fairly significant time to keep creating content every week.

3.7 Amazon KDP

Amazon is the world's leading seller of books. Amazon Kindle is Amazon's service for self-published authors. Amazon allows you to upload and sell ebooks as well as on-demand print books as well. Amazon used to have two different services for self-published authors that they have now consolidated them all under the Kindle umbrella.

Since Amazon is so massive, there are a lot of resources to support people that want to publish on the Kindle platform. There are many examples of courses that will teach you the in's and out's of authoring and selling books on Amazon. If you are going to the effort to produce a video course, it is not that much more effort to format all that material as a book and sell the ebook online. I have personally found that I like to write a book first and then put produce a video course based on the material in the book. This allows me to deliver a much more complete course in a video format since I've already done all the research for the videos by writing the book.

I don't think this is a necessary step for all people and you may find it is perfectly adequate for you to produce course videos and not write an accompanying book. Many people genuinely dislike writing books and producing videos proves to be a much simpler process for them. I have found for me that I enjoy writing books and I also enjoy creating videos I simply of combine the two methods for my coursework.

The revenue share for Amazon for an ebook is either 30% or %70. If you price your ebook under $9.99, you can get a 70% Revenue share from Amazon. The minimum price for an ebook on Amazon is $2.99. If you price your ebook outside of that range, you will get a 30% Revenue share. So for example, if you sell a book for $9.99 under the 70% Revenue share, you will get about $7. There are also distribution fees on top of the revenue split, and this is dependent on the size of your book.

They have an online calculator that will tell you your Revenue split before you publish your book. My experience with publishing on the Amazon platform has been very positive.

3.8 Draft to Digital

Draft2digital is a book aggregator. With a book aggregator, you can publish your book to one site, and they will, in turn, publish your book to a large number of online bookstores. Draft2digital currently publishes books to the following sites:

- Amazon
- Apple Books
- Barnes & Noble
- Kobo
- Playster
- Scribd
- Tolino
- 24Symbols
- OverDrive
- bibliotheca
- Baker & Taylor

Draft2digital will take a fee with each sale that you make and then send you a monthly check based upon your sales. If you publish to

Amazon directly, you cannot use Draft2Digital to publish the same book through this channel. Draft2Digital currently only works with ebooks and does not service hard copy books.

In addition to their book aggregation service, Draft2Digital also offers a simplified way to upload documents that you can quickly turn into ebooks. I have found however if you have a large number of Graphics or complicated formatting requirements you will need to format your ePub book for distribution on this platform.

3.9 Ingram Spark

Ingramspark is a book aggregator. If you wish to sell your books and get them into bookstores like Barnes & Noble, this may be the best approach to do that. With Ingram Spark, you can self publish a book, and they will list it in their catalog for availability to Market to on-premise bookstores such as Barnes & Noble. IngramSpark can publish both ebooks and print books as well. With print books, they will print them on demand as their customers order them from their catalog. There is a fee of $49 for each book that you set up to be in the catalog.

They will offer your books at discounted prices to attract bookstores to buy your books. There are printing and distribution fees for books and an online calculator to help you determine what your profit will be on an individual book. As a ballpark example, if you sell a book for around $15, you will probably make a profit of approximately $3 for each book that you sell.

The good news with this distribution and delivery is that you don't have to be involved in the ordering and shipping process IngramSpark takes care of all that and will also help or your books to their potential buyers.

3.10 Summary

My initial goals for teaching online was to have my own platform for delivering courses. But over time I have found that I can make more money utilizing platforms like Udemy and Skillshare as well as YouTube. The choice, however, is entirely up to you and all of the packages that I've mentioned here are excellent choices for delivering online content. You will have to try some of these to see which one suits your needs the best. In my opinion, self-hosting makes more sense if you have a group of instructors that are producing a lot of content and this way you can begin to drive a significant amount of traffic to a self-hosting platform and make enough money to make it worthwhile.

4 What Should I Teach?

"The three great essentials to achieve anything worthwhile are, first, hard work, second, stick-to-itivness; third, common sense."

Thomas A Edison

What ?

If you have thought about teaching online, you have probably already thought about what you would like to teach. Perhaps you have developed some expertise through your day job that you could leverage by developing courses on the side to make extra income. The other thing you might leverage is a hobby that you have taken up and have an interest in teaching. Whatever the case, if you go out to sites like http://udemy.com and search for course, there is an unbelievable number of classes that are available. Don't be discouraged by this; because of sites like this, there is a considerable demand for courses such as these.

An excellent way to start is to look at a site like Udemy and look for similar courses that you would consider doing your own version. You might consider signing up for one of these courses to get a feel for the material and how the author delivers the content. After taking one of these courses, it will give you some ideas on how to put your spin on it.

Another tool you can leverage from Udemy is a page they call Market Insights. This page will allow you to search courses by topic to evaluate the demand for that topic within the Udemy site as well as the average income for that topic and the top and come within that topic as well. If you look at the snapshot below, I've entered a topic that I am interested in which is a software development topic called web services.

What course topic are you interested in?

WebService ✕

View topic results for courses taught in:

✓ English Spanish ⓘ

Opportunity overview for English courses on **WebService**

🔥 This topic is a great opportunity!

Create Your Course

Student demand	Number of courses	Median monthly revenue	Top monthly revenue
high	low	$126	$446
		per month	per month

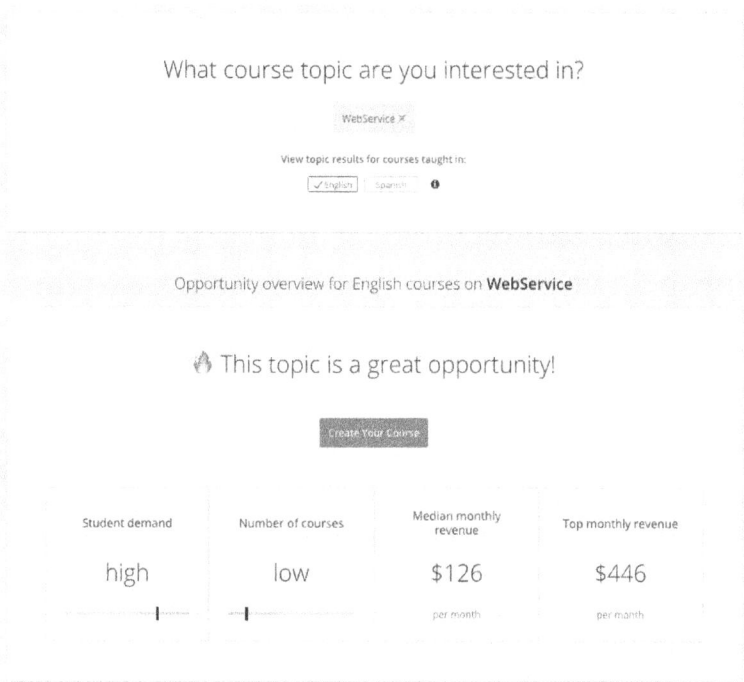

If you look at this screenshot, the median monthly revenue for these courses is $126 in the top-earning instructor earns $446 a month. The report also says that the student demand for this topic is high and there is currently a low number of courses thereby making it an excellent opportunity for a new class. Looking at this type of sight and also looking through the course catalog can give you an excellent idea of some good topics to start with even if you don't intend to launch a course on Udemy this is a great tool to use. You should know however that this tool is only available to instructors. You can sign up to be an instructor for no charge on the Udemy website. Signing up to be an instructor is probably worthwhile just to get access to this tool.

Another thing to consider is your level of interest in the topic you intend to teach. The subject matter should be something that you enjoy because your passion for the area will show through in your course delivery. If it's a topic, you don't enjoy publishing course material will be difficult since it will become more of a chore than something you look forward to doing.

Another thing to consider is the depth of the material that you're considering teaching. It's a good idea to pick a topic that has a lot of material that you can cover in multiple classes. In this way, you can start with a shorter introduction to the area and then expand to intermediate and advanced topics.

Not all subject matter has this type of depth of material. However, if you can find this type of topic, it will make things much easier to deliver smaller shorter courses that are very focused.

Online courses tend to be one of several types:

- Introductory courses
- Deep dive courses
- A Master Class

Introductory courses tend to be reasonably short (less than two hours of material) and focus on getting a student started in a particular subject matter in a short amount of time. Deep dive courses take a specific topic in a very narrow and focused way and thoroughly explain all the details of that topic. These courses tend to be between 2 and 6 hours of video. Master classes present a large amount of detail in one particular subject area and cover it from beginning to end. These courses tend to be more than 10 hours of video and can be extremely long.

I recommend starting with an introductory course in the subject area that you intend to use to start your online business. This way you can test your course delivery method with a shorter course and not risking a significant investment in time with your very first course. It also gives you an opportunity to then sell your next class to the students of your first course and began to develop a following.

If you intend to launch your first course on the Udemy site, courses must have a minimum of five lectures and at least 30 minutes of video content. It may be tempting to offer your first course as a free course. However, I don't recommend this as it will lessen the value of your content in the student's mindset. Instead of a site like Udemy, you can generate coupons that you can give away free access to a paid course. I have found that this is a much better way to create interest in your course while preserving the value of your content.

5 What Equipment Will I Need?

"And now that you don't have to be perfect, you can be good."
John Steinbeck

The picture above is the equipment that I use for my recordings for Linux Academy. One of the great things working for them is they provided me with all the necessary equipment to record my classes. I also have a studio at home that I use for recording my Destin Learning and YouTube videos. My setup at home is not as nice as the equipment I have pictured above, but it gets the job done. Even though the photo above features some high-end equipment, the good news is you can start with very simple equipment and work your way up as you need to. For the very first videos, you shoot you probably already own the only thing you need to get started, a smartphone such as an Android or iPhone. I shot many of my original YouTube and Udemy videos using my iPhone and had decent results. Even the microphone on the iPhone produced credible results for videos. However, in the next section, I am going to recommend using an external video even when you are just starting. Recording quality audio is essential when producing online content. Fortunately, there are some very affordable options for buying a decent microphone to get started.

5.1 Microphone

One of the most important aspects of recording video is sound. Having a quality microphone and set up for sound is probably the most crucial issue for recording videos. If you have lousy sound, you will immediately get bad reviews on your videos. Fortunately, you do not have to spend a lot of money to get a quality microphone. When I first started shooting videos, I used the mic on my iPhone. You can certainly use a cellphone to start off shooting video, but at some point, you should invest some money for a better microphone.

The first upgrade that I used for recording was the Samson Go Mic. This microphone is pictured below. It is a USB portable condenser microphone and is very inexpensive. This microphone cost around $30 and is very small which is great if you intend to record any video while traveling. Using an inexpensive microphone such as this may be a significant first upgrade for your recording equipment.

After using the portable microphone for some time, I upgraded to a better condenser mic. I decided to purchase the Blue Yeti microphone that is pictured below. I did a considerable amount of research, and some people that I followed on YouTube and Udemy recommended this microphone. I have not been disappointed with the Blue Yeti; it does an excellent job and is very versatile. Perhaps the only downside is the yeti is a very sensitive microphone, and it can pick up a lot of sound including background noise. If you have a noisy environment, this may not be the best solution for you as it will pick up background noise.

The last microphone I present here is a much higher end option and is the microphone that I use for my Linux Academy certification videos. This microphone is the Rode Procaster Dynamic vocal microphone. This product is fantastic, and it does not pick up any background noise at all in addition to working well in a very noisy environment. The only downsides of this microphone are it requires a stand, and it is relatively expensive (about $350) for the entire setup. Also, to use this type of microphone, you need to be very close to the equipment when recording. I found the best distance is about 4 inches away from the mic. If you are considering recording videos that you do not want the microphone to be visible in the recording, this is not a good choice for that type of video. However, if you have a considerable volume and you are recording full time, this microphone is an excellent choice.

5.2 Video Cameras

The primary requirement for shooting videos is an HD camera and a tripod. I started off using my iPhone with a simple tripod and then downloaded that video to my Mac for editing. The iPhone (and Android phones) shoot high-quality videos and work well for receding of all types. Also, the nice thing about using a cellphone and a small tripod is that it is very portable. I have packed up my notebook computer, cell phone, and tripod and have recorded many videos while traveling. Pictured below is the setup I used for some of my Destin Learning Videos that I have shot using my cell phone. One of the pieces of software I used when I was getting started is a teleprompter app that I could use to script my videos. This app is called PromptSmart, and you can get information on the app here:

https://promptsmart.com/

Apple iPhone on Tripod

When you continue to progress with your video needs, there is a couple of different ways you could go after using the cell phone. Pictured below is a Canon HD Video camera. One of the create times about this camera is you can flip the preview screen so you can fill in selfie mode at high resolution. You can film videos in selfie mode with most cell phones, but generally, the front-facing camera is not as good as the rear-facing video. When you are recording videos that you appear in it is nice to have a live video screen so you can see in real time what your facial expressions look like while you are recording. This capability cuts down on the amount of rework that any video clip might need.

Canon HT R700 Video Camera

5.3 Video Capture Card

Another great time saver is a video capture card. If you are shooting a lot of videos that you want to include your picture on (as opposed to just using voice-overs to describe slides and diagrams.) A video capture card can stream the imagers real time into your video recording software. Using a video capture card saves the step of saving the video on your camera and then downloading it onto your computer for editing.

Pictured below is a video capture card that I use with my Canon HD camera for filming videos. It is a great time saver and allows me to record a longer amount of video on a single take. You will not need this when you first get started, but once you start using this, you will see a significant boost in your productivity. These devices cost about $200 on Amazon.

AGPTek Video Capture Card

5.4 Lights

If you're going to appear in your videos, you will need to have proper lighting to produce a decent recording. The gold standard for lighting is to use a three-point lighting model. In this lighting model, you have a key light and the fill light that are in front of you and then a backlight behind you to round out and balance the lighting. If you don't have the money to spend on three light stands, you can generally get away with two, provided you have good overhead light wherever you are recording. In my home studio, I mounted some canister lights to the ceiling with CFL bulbs in them that produce a very decent shade of light. These lights in addition to some good overhead lighting allow me to shoot in a well-lighted environment.

If you have a little bit more budget to spend, you can utilize some stand lights better a bit more flexible but take up more floor space wherever you're shooting. In my equipment with my Linux Academy job, I use two stand lights that provide excellent lighting. These light stands are also adjustable so you can adjust the intensity and shade of the light. These lights are probably overkill when you're first getting started, but once you get going, you may opt to reinvest some of your revenue and better lighting. The stand lights that I use daily for pictured below. I've included a link for these in the teaching resources section.

GVM LED Stand Light

5.5 Computer

The good news with my advice on computers is, you can use just about any computer to get started. If you are going to produce a lot of videos you will need to upgrade to a faster processor; otherwise, your production and rendering time will be very slow. I don't recommend upgrading your computer until after you have produced a few videos to see how it goes with the machine you may already have. When I first started creating my videos, I used a PC that I had, and over time I decided to change over to the Mac platform. I was already using an iPhone for my cell phone and changing over to the Mac just made sense for me. I won't get into the Mac vs. PC debate here. I think either the platforms will work for producing videos. I just found for me that I had a personal preference for the Mac.

I have also found that over time with computers becoming much faster than you can use a notebook computer for producing videos with no problem. However to do this, you will need to have a relatively fast notebook computer, and it's also helpful to have a notebook computer that can support an external monitor. In my full-time set up with Linux Academy, I used two external 4K monitors that are hooked up to my MacBook Pro notebook computer. I have found that this is the ideal setup for producing videos. In my home studio that I use for producing Destin Learning videos, I use an iMac with a small external monitor on a stand that I use as a stage monitor. The setup also works very well.

My last piece of advice concerning a computer is to have a large amount of RAM this helps with the video rendering process which is very compute-intensive. 8 GB is the minimum and 16GB is preferred.

5.6 Video Editing Software

There are many excellent video editing software packages on the market today. I have used two of these extensively. The first one is Camtasia from, and I've used it to produce most of my videos for my Destin Learning website. The other package that I use for Linux Academy is ScreenFlow – also an excellent package. Both of these software packages are very similar, and I don't see any differences between the two. It is a personal preference between either of these two packages. They are also both relatively reasonably priced and you can pick either one of these up for around $100.

The other option if you considering using the Mac is iMovie. iMovie is an Apple product and comes standard with any Mac and is a very capable editing package. iMovie is very easy to use, and there is a lot of material on the web that can help you with any detailed questions.

There are also higher-end options for video editing software as well. Adobe Premiere is one of these packages and offers many advanced features for producing videos. This package, however, is a bit more expensive and it requires a longer learning curve to become proficient with it. This package is now part of Adobe Creative Cloud and has many different pricing options that you can buy on a subscription model. I have included links for all of these products in the resources section of this book.

6 Getting Started

"Whatever you can do, or dream you can, begin it. Boldness has genius, power, and magic in it."
Johann Wolfgang Goethe

In this chapter, I am going to talk about one of the most challenging tasks in any project—getting started. The publishing business, in particular, has an associated stigma about getting started. Most people have trouble with the dreaded first book. Although most students have done plenty of writing in their school career, especially those of us that have attended graduate school, writing a book or producing a video course is very difficult for many people to finish. For some reason closing out and publishing the first book for many people seems like an almost impossible task. I think for most of us the fear of failure or the fear of rejection causes us to delay the process. In reality, getting the first book out of the way is the only way to begin to improve as an author. Until you get a product out there, you have nothing to sell, and until you get some feedback, you will not know where you need to improve.

One area that is difficult for all of us has to deal with negative feedback. Especially in the beginning when you are prone to making lots of mistakes, you will likely get a considerable amount of it. It's difficult not to get mad or upset about this but realize that every author including world-famous ones made many mistakes while getting started and had to deal with a lot of negative feedback. I still have a lot of difficulties in dealing with very harsh reviews of my content. However, I have tried to learn as much as I can from negative feedback to improve my content. I often look back at my early material, and I am surprised how poor it seems in comparison to my most recent content. I think you will find that you get better incrementally over time as you produce more and more content whether that's books, videos or online lessons.

Another challenging area for first-time course authors is filming their first videos. Seeing yourself on film or onscreen for the first time is difficult for most people. Most of us are very uncomfortable for the first time on film, and it takes a while to get used to seeing yourself on screen. One strategy I found that it is good to help lessen this, is not to appear for large amounts of time on many of the videos that you film in the beginning. For many types of courses, you can start with having slides from PowerPoint or Google slides for the material that you are covering in the background of the video and you only need to do voice-overs to describe the content. You may need to appear with your face on the video in the introduction or summary. This technique makes the task much more comfortable while you're getting used to filming and seeing yourself on screen. Another method that can lessen that impact is to edit the video in such a way that your face is only visible in a small corner of the screen which seems to reduce the effect of most people's fear of being on video. These are a couple of strategies it might help you when you get started with your filming portion of your courses.

One of the best ways to get started with online teaching is to start a YouTube channel. When you first start a YouTube channel, you will not get a lot of views on your videos, and it will be challenging to grow your channel to a decent size. Also, you won't make a lot of money initially on YouTube. However, YouTube is the second largest search engine in the world and has an incredibly huge audience. You will get immediate feedback on the quality of your content, and it's a great place to start to build a following. You will not be able to monetize your content until you have a thousand subscribers. Although that sounds like a considerable number, the way to start growing is the first get all of your friends and family to subscribe to your channel so that your channel will begin to grow and gain some momentum.

Another great thing about having your material on YouTube is you can take selected videos from your courses and place them online and add a trailer at the end that will advertise your paid version of the course. You can also put links to coupons inside the video descriptions on YouTube. I highly recommend leveraging this platform as a way to get started in the online course business. You will also get a feel for the popularity of various topics that you intend to teach by posting selected videos on numerous content areas on YouTube and gauging the response in terms of the number of views.

Publishing large amounts of material will require you to establish a work schedule it allows you to release content regularly. This schedule will be difficult when you first get started as many tasks will be unfamiliar to you such as writing blog posts or filming videos. You will become much more proficient with these tasks over time, but the most important thing, in the beginning, is to establish a regular schedule where you work on your material on a routine basis.

It's much better to work on material a little bit at a time and to be able to publish courses and videos regularly than it is to try to schedule some type of binge session where you try to put out massive amounts of content very quickly. It may make sense however once you start producing videos to film them in batches as there is some setup time required to do this and is a bit more efficient to create several videos at one time.

Especially for your first course and even on an ongoing basis try to set daily goals for your project or weekly goals if that is your cadence. By doing this, you can get a little bit done each day. If you do this, you will be shocked by the amount of material that you can produce in several months or even over a year. To make a decent amount of money publishing and teaching online, you will need to develop the capability to produce content on a routine basis. One of the metrics that YouTube uses to evaluate channels is the regular cadence that channels have with delivering new content. Most YouTubers will tell you that you will need to deliver new YouTube videos every week at a minimum to be successful on YouTube. I'm not suggesting that you need that type of delivery for online courses, but it is essential that you stick to a regular schedule so that you see sustained growth in your business which will keep you motivated.

In summary in this section, I have talked about some of the items that you should consider to get started with your online teaching business. I have presented some ideas that will hopefully be helpful to you to get started and begin ramping up your online content. I think the best way to get started is beginning with something simple like writing a white paper about the topic you are interested in teaching. You can post your white paper on a website and see what type of interest you get. You can also film a couple of short videos and post them on a YouTube channel and then get feedback from people you know in that particular field. Don't worry if your first content seems rough or you get negative feedback; it's all part of getting started, and everyone has to start somewhere. So don't delay and get started today!

7 Teaching Tips

"Those who know, do. Those that understand, teach."
Aristotle

TEACHING
Tips

In this section, I will describe some things I have learned while teaching and publishing online. I hope these tips can help you avoid some of the mistakes I have made along the way and can make you more successful. Many of these tips seem very simple, but often these are the best kind of advice. Unfortunately, you can only get better at something by practicing so don't be afraid to make mistakes; the most important thing is to jump in and get started.

7.1 Tools

My first tip to you is to use either Google Docs or Microsoft Office 365 to develop your material so you have one place that you can go to edit either books that you are developing, PowerPoint slides or notes for your business. I now use Google Docs for everything and have found it to be outstanding–particularly for collaboration and sharing documents with other people who help me review my content. I no longer have to email attachments all over the place and then consolidate those comments back into the original text. The capability that Google Docs has to share documents with people has saved me an enormous amount of time and has increased my ability to produce more content dramatically.

My second tip is to use a service like Grammarly to help proof your content. Grammarly offers a free service that you can use to get started, but for a minimal investment, you can upgrade to the paid version which will help you produce higher quality content and to help to scrub out those annoying typos and grammatical errors. I have found that the spell checker in Microsoft Word not to be very effective at catching many problems. Once I moved to Grammarly, I was able to produce higher quality content at a faster rate.

One of the limitations of being a small business is that you do not have many resources two directed various projects. Another limitation at least for me is that I don't have a huge budget to hire out an army of contractors to help me get things done. One thing I have found that is helping me get things done is to use contractors on Fiverr. I have contracted out tasks to develop book covers, course images, and basic editing tasks. Most of the services on Fiverr are very reasonably priced, and you can find people that do outstanding work. One contractor I use in particular (Pro eBook Covers) has delivered some amazing book covers for me. I have a link to her service in the appendix of this book. I highly recommend her work.

Another tip concerning tools – I use Canva to develop some of my supporting graphics for my coursework. Canva is free to use and offers many templates that can give you ideas for graphics you are trying to develop in support of your courses.

The last tip I have with essential tools is to use software like Handbrake to compress your videos after production. By compressing these videos, you have much smaller files to work with, and it is faster to upload to your target platforms such as YouTube or Udemy. Handbrake is free to use and install, and I've included a link for the that in the appendix of this book.

7.2 Marketing Your Content

Marketing my content for my online business has been the most challenging aspect to get started. I am a technical person by nature, and I have minimal hands-on marketing experience. Also, much of the technology has changed rapidly over the last few years, and online marketing is quite a bit different than traditional marketing techniques that were common even just a few years ago. I have found a couple of things that have really helped me and have been successful for me so far.

The first of these is YouTube. I've had quite a bit of success with my YouTube channel, and it has assisted me in growing my business and establishing my online presence. I highly recommend and if you're going to do online courses to start with YouTube so that you can get a feel for what content students are looking for and you also get early feedback on the quality of your content. I've also found that by posting portions of my classes online I can put links for my paid content on YouTube and I've had some success and getting conversions from those links.

The other tip I have is to set up a full suite of social media sites such as Facebook Instagram and Twitter. The problem with delivering content to all these sites is it's very labor-intensive to do it on a manual basis. I recommend using a tool like HootSuite where you can post your material and schedule it in one place, and it automates delivering content to all of those social media platforms. HootSuite is very reasonably priced, and I have a link for that tool in the appendix of this book.

7.3 General Tips

One of the temptations you have early on when you start your teaching business is to give away a large amount of free content to draw in users for your courses or your website. Initially, you may get some interested students, but I have found the people that sign up for free content generally do not engage in courses and are not good long-term prospects for customers. For me, a better approach for this is to give out coupons to classes that have substantial discounts to bring people in or perhaps give out a limited number of free coupons, but offering content for free such as books or courses has generally not worked for me in the long term.

Another tip I have for creating videos is to try not to script your content. Even if you don't appear on screen if you read a script, your audience can tell that you are reading and it hurts your delivery. What I found is a practical approach to this is not to have a script, but to have a series of notes that are bullet points to outline the topics that I am discussing so that I don't forget anything and that I include all the relevant information. This approach seems to to be a much better than scripting and a conversational tone in your videos has a much more convincing effect on your students.

My last tip concerning video production is it's essential to practice your video content before filming especially for the first videos that you shoot — spending an extra five or ten minutes just rehearsing the video before your film saves you an enormous amount of time and editing. The last tip is, you need to have an engaging voice while you're delivering your video. Even if you think you're upbeat and engaging, you need to step it up a notch so that this comes through in the recorded content. The last thing students want to hear is a tired, hung-over voice that has been out way too late the night before!

7.4 Summary

In this section, I have presented some of the common sense tips that I have learned over the last few years while developing online content and writing books. Even if some of these tips sound very simple, combining them all can save you quite a bit of time and help you move your business forward. I hope that some of these tips work out well for you and that you have great success in your online teaching business.

8 Marketing Your Classes

"Know thyself. Know the customer. Innovate."
Beth Comstock

In this chapter, I will discuss some techniques to market your classes. I will warn you right up front that I am not a marketing guru and I don't have a magic method for making you rich quick. I have, however, been able to steadily grow my business and increase the speed at which I can deliver content. Some of these methods have been more successful for me than others. I will point these out along the way.

YouTube

I have had the most successful marketing my material on YouTube to this point. I also really enjoy releasing video content on YouTube as well. YouTube is the second largest search engine in the world behind Google search. You can annotate your videos with popup messages that you can use to market your material. You can also put links in the video descriptions as well. As you gain subscribers on your channel, you will see more view on each video you release. This method, however, is a long process and will take some time to grow your channel. When you are just getting started, this process may be frustrating. If you stick with it and publish material regularly, you will see long term growth.

Email List

One of the best ways to market your course materials is through email if you decide to have your own website. (I recommend that you do.) You can place a sign-up form on your site for newsletters and more information about your site. I use SumoMe for that signup process; it is an excellent tool and offers a free level to get started.

Once you start building your email list, you will need a tool to send you messages to your list. I started with a free account with MailChimp. They have an excellent service, and it is easy to use. After using this for some time, I switched over to MailerLite. They have some extra features I was looking for and were a bit cheaper than MailChimp. I will tell you that I really don't like sending out email, but it is a part of the business that is necessary to build repeatable sales. I have included links to both MailChimp and MailerLite in the Teaching Resources later in this book.

Facebook

Another way to market your content is to build a Facebook page. You can post some of your content here along with marketing materials. It is straightforward to set up a Facebook business page and to publish material. You can also run ads from Facebook, but it is a bit more complicated to set up. I have not had the greatest success with Facebook ads, but I have learned much more about it, and my more recent ads on this platform have been getting better results.

Google Ads

Google is the king of internet marketing. With Google ads, you can set up search ads, video ads and display ads. I was able to grow my YouTube channel substantially through the use of Google ads. While the potential of Google Ads is incredible, it is a complicated platform to learn and master. There are many excellent courses on Udemy that you can take to get up to speed with this, but it will take a significant time investment to make progress with this. I have committed to this and am slowly improving with this incrementally.

LinkedIn

LinkedIn is an excellent platform for you to market your course materials, particularly if you have some business connections that might benefit from your material. I have not run ads on LinkedIn to this point as most of my business connections are more in the software management area and are not my target audience.

Coupon Sites

If you are planning to sell courses on Udemy, there as many coupon sites that you can place discount coupons for your classes. You will get a much better revenue share when sales come from your coupons. You will get 97% of a sale from your coupons on Udemy. The bad news is you will probably only be able to sell your courses for a maximum of $9.99 per transaction. Udemy changed their pricing structure several years ago, and now they have monthly sales of all classes at $9.99. If you want to sell your courses for a higher price you will probably have to sell them directly on your own website. Having your own website will require you to have a much better handle on marketing. I have included some links to Udemy coupon sites in the resources section of this book.

Summary

I recommend that once you get your business off the ground to devote a percentage of your revenue to a monthly marketing budget to invest in ads. You can also hire out small marketing tasks on Fiverr to help you with some of these tasks. Fortunately, if you start on sites like Udemy and Skillshare or Amazon Kindle, you don't need to invest in marketing right away. You will be able to make organic sales on these platforms since they will help you market your courses. However, without an effective marketing plan, you will not be able to grow your business fast enough to become a full-time income.

9 Course Production Process

In this chapter, I'm going to describe the high-level process of creating a course. You do not have to follow this process step by step, and it is possible to do many of these steps in parallel. I have found it much better for me to follow a step-by-step process that is repeatable. Following this process helps me create content on a regular, predictable schedule. The following figure describes the significant steps in this process. In the remainder of this chapter, I describe some of the details of each of these steps as well as some tips to help you speed up the process.

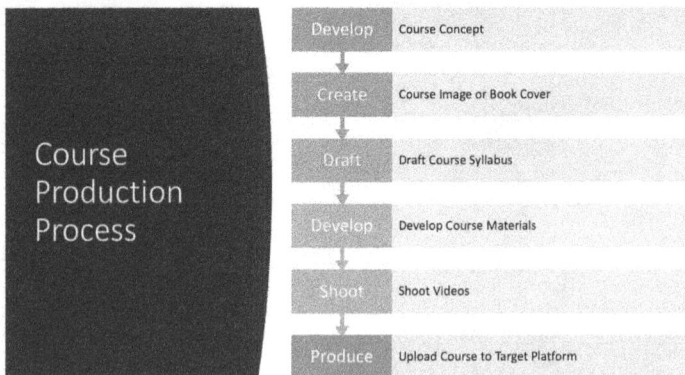

Course Production Process

Develop	Course Concept
Create	Course Image or Book Cover
Draft	Draft Course Syllabus
Develop	Develop Course Materials
Shoot	Shoot Videos
Produce	Upload Course to Target Platform

9.1 Course Concept

The first step of the process is to develop a course concept which is the overall idea of what you intend to present in the course. You can start by looking at sites like Udemy and Skillshare to see what classes are already available and if they are popular or not. At this point, you can also to begin to think about the course title and some of the high-level material that you think you would like to include. During this time you can also look at the Udemy marketplace insights to get an idea if this topic is popular and what the potential demand for the course might be. Again, even if there are already a lot of classes in the marketplace for your particular topic, you might be able to put a fresh spin on it and market your course in a way, and you can gain market share in that particular domain. This process does not need to be a one-time event. I keep notes on lots of different course ideas I have and store them in a spreadsheet, and I then refer to from time to time as I develop ideas.

9.2 Create a Course Image

The next step is to create a course image for your course. In terms of the production process, you could always do this at a later time, but I like to do this, in the beginning, as this process helps me further refine the material I'm going to have in the course. If I am writing a book, I will develop the cover at this point as well. The image of the class or publication helps me to concentrate on the overall material of the course, and it also gives me a feeling of accomplishment so that I can begin the detailed course production process in the right frame of mind. If you are not very artistically inclined, I recommend that you hire this process out. If you are developing a course for Udemy, they will provide you with a course image for you to use free of charge. Even if you intend to design your graphic, you may want to have them develop one to help you with ideas for your version.

9.3 Course Syllabus

After you have developed the course concept and course image, it is now time to put the details of all the material in a course syllabus. The syllabus should include all of the sections of the class as well as identifying any hands-on activities or labs that you want to integrate within the course. You should arrange your syllabus in terms of significant sections or chapters and then individual lessons within each of those chapters. If you are developing a video course, you should indicate whether each lesson is a video, a lab, or a text article that you will place in the class as supporting material. We will look at developing the syllabus and much more detail in creating your first-course section of this book.

9.4 Develop Course Materials

During this phase of the production process, you will develop any supporting materials for your course. These materials include lab exercises source code if you are developing a computer programming class and any content that you intend to present to students that they can download as part of the course. Depending on the type of course that you are developing, this can be a significant portion of the production process. I have found over time at producing high-quality supporting materials for teaching and including them when I am developing the syllabus, significantly improves the quality of the course and the learning experience for the students. When you first start developing online courses, you will naturally concentrate on the video portion of the classes. Over time you will find that this process becomes pretty routine and developing the supporting course materials will take more time and creativity to create high-quality courses.

9.5 Shoot Videos

Now it is time in the process to record video lessons after you have produced the supporting material. Even though I have laid out this process sequentially, you have two choices for video production. The first option is to develop all the supporting material first before you shoot all the videos. This process can make the video production process much shorter since you have things all ready to go. The other option is to produce the material for one lesson and then go ahead and shoot the video for that lesson and cycle through the syllabus one lesson at a time. This way you can alternate between producing content and shooting videos. I prefer writing all the content first and then filming all the videos at one time, but if I'm developing a very long and complicated course, this can become tiring—and I sometimes move to cycle through one lesson at a time to break up the monotony. Also, if you are considering authoring a book, I recommend writing the book first and then doing the video course. For me this is much easier since the book contains all the information and then producing the videos is a straightforward process.

9.6 Produce Videos

The last step in the process is to produce your videos and upload them to your target platform. This step involves rendering your final videos from your editing software into a format such as MP4 that you can upload to YouTube, Udemy or skillshare. You will also want to compress your videos at this point using a tool such as Handbrake that I described earlier in this book. If you are producing a course for Udemy, it will also need to go through a review process before your course can go up for sale. This process may take a couple of days so plan for that in your process. Other platforms such a Skillshare or YouTube do not have any review process, and you can release material right away. This step is also a perfect time for you or someone else you know to review the videos for any potential errors or issues so that you can catch these before your course goes into production.

In summary, in this chapter, we have reviewed the overall production process to put together a video class and produce it to an online platform such as Udemy. In the next chapter, we will discuss in detail each one of these steps, and we will go through the exercise of producing various portions have your first class in a step-by-step way.

10 Create Your First Course

In this chapter, I will take you through the exercise that I went through in creating this course, and you can use this as a guideline for your course and create similar products step by step for your course. At this point, you should be well on your way to creating your first class once this exercise is complete.

10.1 Course Concept

The first thing to start with is a course concept. While you are formulating your idea, you can look at similar courses on sites like Udemy or Skillshare for ideas. For this course, I used Lucidchart to create a series of Post-it notes that had some of the ideas that I wanted to include in this course. You don't need to use an online tool for this, but I found this easier for me since I could access it anywhere and didn't have to work in a particular location. I've included a snapshot of what this chart looks like, and I intend to use this method in the future for other courses as I put the ideas together. Sometimes I have ideas about classes that I will publish much later down the road, and it's good to have a place to record these ideas once I have them; otherwise, I will forget them. I have included a link to Lucidchart in the resources section of this book.

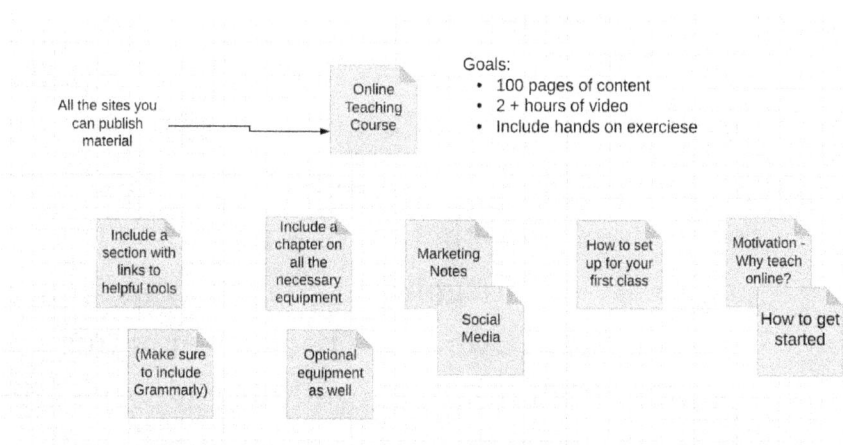

You can also use a mind map for this process as well or just a piece of paper and start drawing out your ideas. I am a very visual learner and for me using a method like Post-it notes or drawing on a whiteboard helps me with the creative process. At this stage, try to be as complete as possible with all of your ideas and then you can formulate them into groups and chapters and subchapters later on in the process.

10.2 Course Image

After you have created your course concept, the next step is to create an image for your course. The platform you intend to publish on such as Udemy will dictate some of the requirements for this image. For example, Udemy requires that there is no text on the image. If you are going to create a book, you will also need to create a book cover at this point as well. It is technically not necessary to publish these covers at this point in the process; you only really need them once you are ready to publish to your platform. The reason I like to do it at this point is it helps me further with the creative process, and I begin to think of the entire product that I'm trying to produce at this point.

I have included an example of producing it an image that I used for this course on Canva. Let's take a look at some of the details of creating a course image in Canva.

First, go to the following website:

http://www.canva.com

Next, sign up for a free account in the following sign up block:

Design anything. Publish anywhere.

Create an account, it's free. Canva is loved by beginners and experts, teams and individuals.

Name

Tell us what you do ⌄

We'll use this info to help you get the most out of Canva.

f Facebook	G Google

Sign up with email

By signing up, you agree to Canva's Terms of Use and Privacy Policy.

After you have signed up you should see the
following screen:

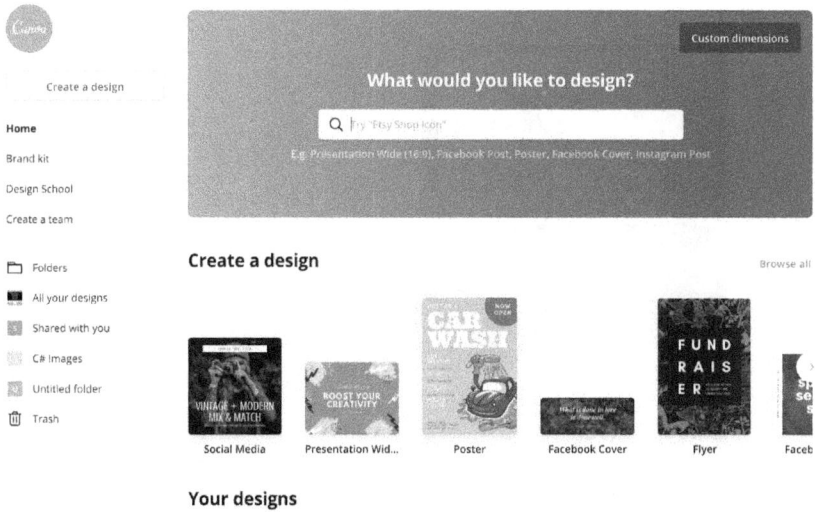

Click on the custom dimensions button in the
upper right-hand corner and use the
dimensions 750 x 433, the designated pixel
ratio size for a course image in Udemy.

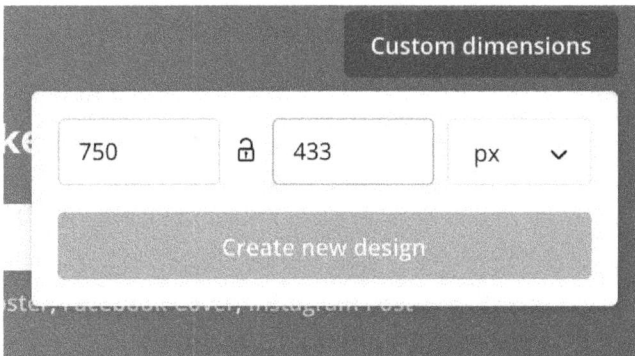

You should now see a screen like the
following:

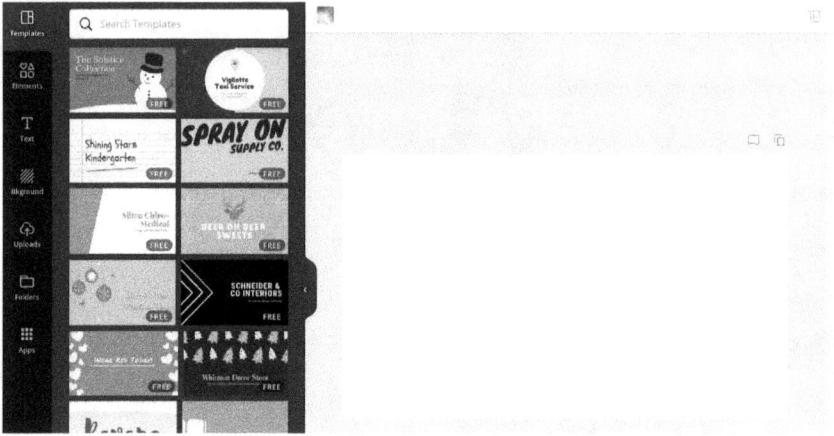

First set the background of the image by clicking on the background button on the left-hand side. I have selected a blue background in the screenshot below. There are many image background selections available. There are also some paid images you can use as well.

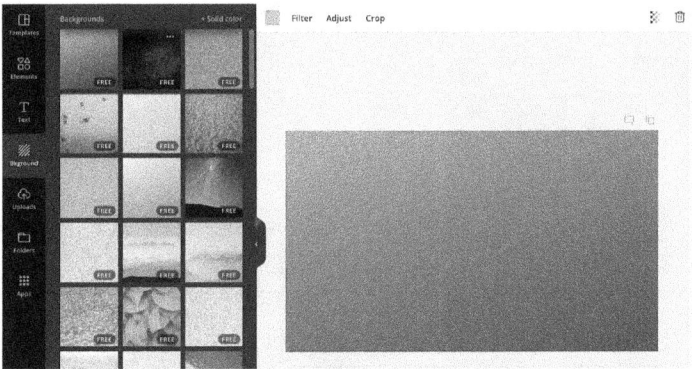

After you've set the background, you can draw whatever you want on the canvas using the tools on the left-hand toolbar. You can also upload images as well from your local computer. I will show this in the next step in the screenshot below, where I have dragged in a teacher image from a graphic image that I uploaded from my computer.

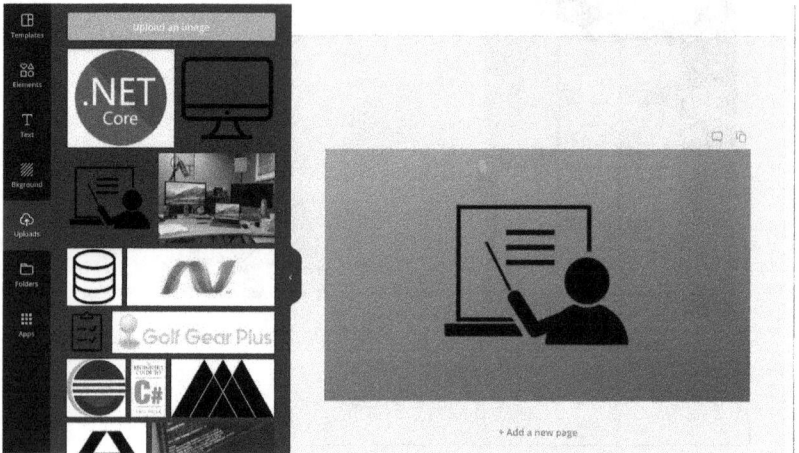

There are also many other operations you can do at this point such as including text, drawing basic shapes, and changing colors. However, for this discussion, I'm going to leave this as a simple example for you to follow for you to create your course image. At this point, you can now download the image to your computer so that you can upload it to Udemy or wherever you are going to teach when you are ready to start uploading materials to your course platform. To do this click on the downloads menu selection from the publish menu as in the following screenshot.

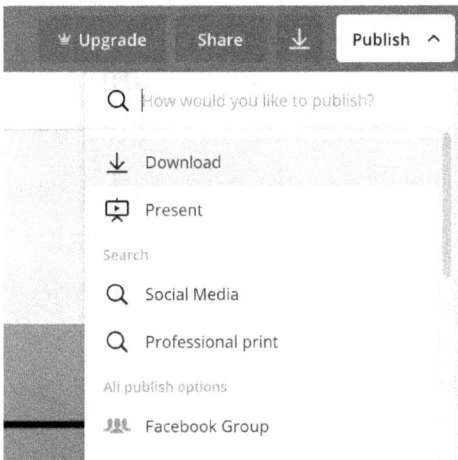

Next, select the file type you would like for
your download a PNG file is fine for most
platforms.

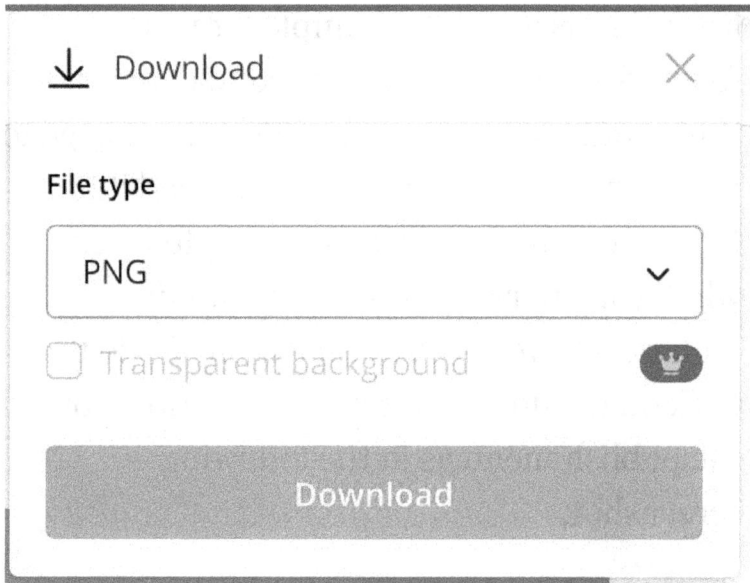

↓ Download	✕

File type

PNG	⌄

☐ Transparent background   👑

Download

Although this is a straightforward example,
you should now have the basics to be able to
create your course image and download it to
your computer. If you are not happy with the
image you create, you can also hire someone
to do it for you on a site like Fiverr.

10.3 Course Syllabus

Now that you have created all the high-level materials for the course you can now produce your course syllabus. The course syllabus is just a detailed outline of all the course contents. It should be a straightforward process now that you have a comprehensive concept and have created an image or book cover that reflects the ideas you've developed in the first step. Listed below is the course syllabus for this class. In reality, it's just the table of contents for this book. When I began full production for this class, I use this as my road map for both writing the book and developing the accompanying videos for this course as well.

10.4 Course Materials

The next step in the process is to create all associated course materials that will go with your videos. These would include hands-on learning activities labs or any downloads that support the course or any other materials that would be outside of a book or video. Other useful items to include in video courses are quizzes or final exams that help reinforce the material presented in the videos. Most online course platforms have online quizzes as a feature of the course. The first step and using these features, however, is to write down all the questions and possible answers. Most platforms support multiple choice types of questions. Depending on the kind of course that you are developing, this can be a very time-consuming part of the process, so you should plan for this in advance in your schedule.

10.5 Shoot Videos

You're now ready to record videos for your courses. You will need to decide what types of shots you would like to include for your video. For your first courses, I recommend you do voice overs from PowerPoint or Google Slides presentations. These are the easiest videos to produce, and it's straightforward to edit the audio portion since your picture is not on screen. You can also start with a talking head video where your picture is in a small corner of the video in the material you are presenting is in the rest of the video. This method is also a good way if you are not that comfortable being on screen since you're only on a small portion of the video. This type of shot will make you much more comfortable being on screen.

You can use a cell phone in selfie mode on a tripod to get started with your first videos. I have included a photo of the setup that I sometimes use in the picture below.

You should break up your videos and several distinct clips and shorter pieces. By having several clips, this will make the video much easier to record. If you are recording from PowerPoint slides you can break up the audio into one slide at a time this will make the editing process much more straightforward. Now that you have shot your videos and recorded them you are now ready for final editing.

10.6 Produce Videos

One of the primary production components of online teaching is video editing. Although it is possible to hire this task out to a company or consultant that can be very expensive when you are first starting, it is not hard to master video editing on your own, but it will take some practice to get good at it and to be able to turn it around quickly. When you first start teaching online, you will see this as a significant time step in producing your courses. After you have been doing it for a while, you will find that researching your classes will take far more time than editing and creating videos.

There are many excellent video editing packages on the market that are pretty simple to use and pretty affordable. Some of these packages include Camtasia, ScreenFlow, iMovie and Adobe Premiere to name a few. I have added links for these software packages in the appendix of this book so that you can go and check them out. If you already work for an educational institution, most of these vendors offer discounts for teachers.

There are also some online video editing sites that you can create a video without installing software on your computer. The only one of these sites that I have used is Adobe Spark. It is a pretty good option to use this for some of your first videos when you're first getting started. They have a free tier option that you can start with that allows you to edit video online as well as overlay royalty free music. The free tier, however, does overlay a watermark on the videos that you produce. This watermark may not be a big deal when you first get started, yet at some point you will want to move away from this.

Most video editing software packages have many of the same features, but what may drive you to a decision is the type of computer platform that you're using. Several years ago I switched over to using a Mac to edit video, and I found it this platform is better for me. I have created some videos on the PC just for my personal preference though I noticed that the Mac worked better for what I was trying to get done. The M, however, is a much more expensive platform than the PC, but I found the extra cost was worth it for the types of videos I was trying to create. Some software packages such as Camtasia are available for both Windows and PCs, but others such as iMovie are only available for the Mac. There are also some open-source video editing software packages that support not only the Mac and the PC but also the Linux operating system. If you are a Linux user, you should try out one of these packages to see if it will meet your needs.

The basic video production process is to film several clips of the subject you are trying to teach. It is best to break up longer lessons into a series of shorter chunks that you can record as separate clips. If you are using PowerPoint or Google Slides as a backdrop for your videos you can record a clip for each slide. Once you have recorded these clips, you can create a project in your video editing software and import each of these clips into your project. After you have imported these clips, you can cut out unwanted portions of each clip, insert transitions between each of the clips for visual effects, and add annotations to highlight various aspects of the material you are presenting.

If you are only recording audio on your video and not including yourself in the picture you can also edit the audio portion of your video to clean up any unwanted sounds such as "ahhs" and "umms," by doing this you can really clean up the presentation of your videos and have a much more professional video.

After you have finished the editing process, you can now save your project and begin the final production process. The final step is to produce your video from your project to the desired target resolution for where you are going to publish your video. The standard for most platforms today is to produce your video in full HD or 1080p. It is during this time that you will notice the speed of your computer as this is a very compute-intensive process. If you have a slow computer, this rendering will take quite some time. Faster processors will render a 10-minute video in a matter of a couple of minutes.

Once this you have completed the rendering process, you are now ready to upload your video to your target platforms such as Udemy or YouTube. However, before doing this, you should compress your video by running it through a tool such as Handbrake. Handbrake is an open source tool that is free to download—an excellent tool to compress videos. Compressing these videos is the best practice, and will save you a lot of storage space as well as cut down on time that it will take to upload videos to your target platform. I've included a link for where you can download handbrake in the appendix of this book.

11 Change the World!

"Education is the most powerful weapon which you can use to change the world."
Nelson Mandela

The thing that I love about teaching and publishing online is that it is a means for me to tell my own story in my own words, and have an opportunity to tell my story to the world. The words are my own, written my way, and precisely in the manner that I wish to relate the story. It is far different than working for a large company and writing their story which is molded and influenced by what your boss has to say.

The downside to that is maybe no one is interested in what you have to say, or it is difficult to market your works. For me, the plus side is I don't have to second-guess the opportunity to start my own business. I much rather have tried something and failed than not having tried at all.

Perhaps an even bigger reason to teach online or even offer praise for that matter, is it is an opportunity to change someone's life for the better. You may think this is a trite statement or an over exaggeration, but I assure you if you publish material long enough it will genuinely impact someone else's life.

After starting at Linux Academy, I attended a professional show, the Google Next Conference. I had just started at the company and was not all that familiar with the company at this point. While working at our sales booth, I was approached by a group of people that told us they were some of our students.

They were very interested in meeting one of our authors who was not at the booth at the moment. I asked them if I could help them in some way. They asked me to pass along their thanks for his certification training classes. They were very grateful to him for putting together a quality product, and they said in fact that they were confident that this certification was key to them getting jobs with their current employer, Google. I was blown away by that statement to think that one of our certification classes had such a massive impact on some of our student's lives.

After returning from that conference, I was later at a company meeting where another group of content authors and salespeople had returned from another show. They had very similar stories to share about the profound impact our courses were having in changing people's lives. You may think these stories are over the top, but I assure these stories are true. In fact, one of Linux Academy's core values is:

"We are committed to changing the world by changing lives."

You might not see this type of impact right away, but know as you are getting started this can be a fantastic end goal to have in mind. If you are on the fence about getting started, I encourage you to give it a try. Figure out a way to get started. Start small and publish your ideas. Stay up late, get up early, work on your weekend, but give your publishing and teaching dream a legitimate shot.

Even if you start small, aim high and change the world!

12 Summary

Thank you so much for reading this book. I hope I have given you some excellent information to provide you with a head start on your online teaching business. Teaching online is a great business, but like anything, it will require hard work and dedication for you to be successful. I sincerely hope that this can be a great success for you and provide you with a business that will allow you a flexible and enjoyable lifestyle.

Thank you again and please be sure and leave a review for this book as I would love to hear from you. Good luck with your adventure of teaching online!

13 Teaching Resources

RESOURCES

This list below is a number of helpful links to help get you started with teaching and publishing online. I have used a number of these resources to get my online business started and continue to find new helpful material online every day. Please also check my webpage for additional resources.

https://www.destinlearning.com/teach

Udemy Teaching Guidelines
https://support.udemy.com/hc/en-us/section
s/360001167193-Course-Material-Basics

Skillshare Teacher Handbook
https://www.skillshare.com/teach/handbook

Teach on Skillshare
https://www.skillshare.com/teach

Kindle Direct Publishing Home
https://kdp.amazon.com/en_US

Kindle Direct Publishing - Getting Started
https://kdp.amazon.com/en_US/help/topic/
G200635650

Thinkific

https://www.thinkific.com/

Teachable

https://teachable.com/

The Quickstart Guide to YouTube

https://creatoracademy.youtube.com/page/course/bootcamp-foundations

Grammarly

https://www.grammarly.com

Video Editing Software

ScreenFlow

https://www.telestream.net/screenflow/overview.htm

Camtasia

https://www.techsmith.com/video-editor.html

iMovie

https://www.apple.com/imovie/

Three Point Lighting Video

https://tubularinsights.com/three-point-lighting-technique/

Recommended Tools

Grammarly

https://www.grammarly.com

Canva   https://canva.com

Handbrake   https://handbrake.fr

Fiverr

https://www.fiverr.com/

pro_ebookcovers

https://www.fiverr.com/pro_ebookcovers

Email Services

MailChimp

MailerLite

14 About the Author

Eric Frick

I have had roles in software development and
information technology operations for 30
years. I have worked as a Software Developer,
Software Development Manager, Software
Architect and as an Operations Manager. For
the last five years, I have taught evening
classes in various Computer Science related
subjects at several local universities. In 2015, I
founded destinlearning.com and developed a
series of online courses and books that can

provide practical information to students on various computer science and software development topics.

I am also a full-time course author for Linux Academy and work on certification training for cloud computing. You can view my classes at http://linuxacademy.com.

You can also visit my author page on Amazon here: https://www.amazon.com/Eric-Frick/e/B01N 17DAZJ

www.ingramcontent.com/pod-product-compliance
Lightning Source LLC
Chambersburg PA
CBHW071702210326
41597CB00017B/2301